The Amazon Self-Publishing Guidebook

Why Your Books Are Not Selling, How To Get Reviews Legitimately, And Updates To The Algorithm

Richard Abbott

Table Of Content

Introduction

Hi!

You've picked up this book either because you've heard about self-publishing books on Amazon and want to learn more or you want to learn how to take your self-publishing business to the next level. In either case, I will tackle all your concerns and give you a clear picture of this business.

My first book 'How To Successfully Self-Publish A Book On Amazon & Audible' has had some great feedback. That book focused on the basics of Amazon KDP, how to find winning keywords, the technicalities of Amazon ads, audiobooks, and more topics. I will be taking a different approach to this book. Since my last book, there have been some important changes on Amazon regarding self-publishing that I would like to address. This book is also a more generic guide on self-publishing and answers some really important questions that beginners often ask and addresses some mistakes that I see beginners often fall into.

After completing this book, you will be more educated on self-publishing and ready to take your business to the next level. I share some valuable insights about self-publishing in this book that I have not shared anywhere else.

In addition, I address the issue that many self-publishers have, which is a need for book sales. I explain why many publishers don't see success with their books, and I give real scenarios to explain my strategy and approach to producing a book that sells consistently.

Chapter 1: Online Courses – Necessary Or A Waste Of Time?

Suppose you've been looking at ways to make money online for a notable time. In that case, you've probably become aware of the popularity of online courses within the last few years that sell for $1000+ and that promise to help you start earning a sizable income on the Internet.

In this chapter, I will discuss what I think of online Amazon KDP courses based on my experience. I will address who I believe an online course is good for, who it's not good for, and my overall verdict on them regarding Amazon KDP.

The first thing that needs to be addressed concerning online courses is that too many people perceive that if they buy an online course, regardless of the skill the course is teaching, they will instantaneously learn to become successful and make money online. Undoubtedly, some courses are valuable, although buying any course is just the first step. What you do after buying the course will be a big determining factor in whether you succeed in that business model. However, buying a course in and within itself does not give you the right to be successful.

What separates a paid course from free material on the Internet?

This is a really good question we must ask ourselves. The answer will actually surprise you.

People think that buying a $1000+ course from a 'guru' will give them an advantage over people consuming free content on the likes of YouTube. I have purchased a few expensive self-publishing courses myself, and I can tell you this is categorically wrong.

A lot of the information on these paid courses is actually widely available on the Internet. This raises another question: why do people invest a lot of money into these courses?

The answer is simple. It comes down to MARKETING! You see, the course creators position themselves in a way where you would feel stupid if you were not to take them up on their offer. The creators are smart and have learned the art of sales. Whether that is through making wild claims of becoming profitable within a short period of time or by sharing screenshots of their earnings and using that as their main selling point, it all comes down to marketing.

I have learned much more from watching YouTube videos of self-publishers compared to the paid content of these courses.

Another important thing to mention is that many of these course creators are not actively publishing books anymore. Their main income is selling you outdated information on publishing books that worked 2/3 years ago.

Think about it for a second.

Why would you sell books online when you can make 10x the money by simply telling other people how to do it?

It is best to start off as a beginner by consuming free content from people who are actively publishing books. Regardless of whether you are in the low content or fiction/non-fiction space, many active YouTubers publish books and upload free content onto YouTube. Taking a paid course would make more sense once you have become more informed about self-publishing.

Who is a course good for?

As I have previously said, all course material is widely accessible on YouTube. With that being said, you may not find all of the information in one neat place. Which brings me to my next topic, who is a course good for?

- A course is good for a person who has a full-time job or is always busy and occupied and has no time to sit and explore free content online. A good course should cover the A-Z of self-publishing in one organized place, and you would go over the content at your own speed.

- A course is good for someone who would like 1 to 1 support or a mentor. One thing I appreciate about these online courses is that most of them have active Facebook groups of other people within the same course with the same goal as you. Courses can be a very effective form of networking with like-minded individuals (ONLY when done properly).

Apart from those two reasons, I would not purchase a paid self-publishing course as a beginner. That $1000+ that you invest into the course could be used to get your first few books written, get graphic designers, book editors, book formatters, and invested into Amazon Ads.

My final verdict: Courses are a luxury, not a necessity

With the information and knowledge that I have now, I would not recommend a beginner to purchase an expensive course. No matter what type of books you want to publish, plenty of self-publishers on YouTube will run you through the process and effective strategies.

If, after reading this, you still would prefer to purchase a course and you don't think YouTube is enough for you, I would advise looking at some of the self-publishing courses on Udemy. They are moderately priced at $50 and less and very lengthy and comprehensive. Just make sure to filter out the ones with great reviews.

Chapter 2: High Content Or Low Content Books?

This is a question that I often see posed by beginners who are still deciding which genre to start with when self-publishing. In this chapter, I will share my views regarding both and conclude which is the most attractive opportunity in my opinion.

Let's start by explaining what the hell high or low content books are.

High-content books are books with a significant amount of text in them. They usually fall in the department of either fiction or non-fiction. A book is usually considered high content by consensus if it is above 20,000 words and usually at least 100 pages in total length, although this depends on the book dimensions you wish to publish with and the font size you go with. Therefore, take these metrics with a pinch of salt.

Low-content books have minimal content in the interior. Examples of low-content books are activities, puzzles, or coloring books. On the other hand, no-content books are books with no content inside them. This includes journals that only have lines for writing or lined notebooks etc.

Which one should I publish?

I have been a self-publisher on Amazon for over 3 years at this stage, and I recommend high-content publishing much more than low-content/no-content publishing.

Let me tell you why.

The barrier to entry for low content is really low

There is a known concept in business: When the barrier to entry is low, the competition is intensive. This statement sums up low content and no contention publishing very well.

Since low/no content books are so easy to pump out, they have become the most competitive types of books on Amazon. Competition is not necessarily bad (I will speak about this later), but as a beginner just getting their hands wet with the business model, you want to give yourself the best possible chance of making notable money with Amazon. By starting out with low-content books, you are making it harder for yourself with all of the competition.

It is common for a low/no content publisher to pump out hundreds of books a month onto Amazon. In my opinion, there are a few things wrong with this:

- Many of these books could be better quality and are knockoffs of previous books already published.
- Making subtle changes to a book and publishing it as a new one is unethical, in my opinion.
- It ruins the reputation of self-publishing.

High-content publishing has a higher earning potential

The barrier to entry for high-content publishing is higher. It requires funds to get started, unlike low-content books, which can be created within a few minutes using software like Canva.

When the barrier to entry is higher, it usually means less competition. As a self-publisher on Amazon for the last few years, there is still a great opportunity for new high-content books in fiction and non-fiction. Every month I come across a dozen untapped keywords with virtually no competition and high demand that would otherwise be very difficult to find in the low/no content space.

Another important thing to mention is that people need to be subject experts to get started with high-content publishing, whether fiction or non-fiction.

While that would be really beneficial, this is optional.

People think that it is 'unethical' and 'wrong' to publish under a fictional pen name and to have your book written by a ghostwriting company or writer with subject expertise in your niche. I disagree with this notion. Are people unaware that many famous authors use esteemed ghostwriting companies to write their work?

Even the ones that don't use a writer, a lot of them still take ideas and inspiration from other people.

As long as the ghostwriter is compensated fairly for their writing efforts, there is nothing unethical or wrong with hiring a ghostwriter.

Regarding earning potential, the likeliness to succeed with a high-content book is much higher than with a low-content book. Low/no content publishers typically have thousands of books on their bookshelf, yet for 97% of them, most of their income is comprised of just a few books. That's a scary approach if you ask me…

Whereas speaking for myself, I only typically publish a new book every few months, and my bookshelf currently, at the time of writing this book, has 10 books in total. The bulk of my income from self-publishing comes from 6-7 books. This approach makes sense and is a lot less risky. Spending quality time on each book and ensuring that you satisfy your market will enable you to have higher chances of making consistent book sales than pumping out hundreds of low-quality books a month and hoping for a few of them to take off.

High-content books are eligible for Kindle Select, whereas low-content books are not

You may be thinking, 'And? Why does that matter?' well, it actually does. Let me tell you why.

Amazon does not allow low/no content books to be published in e-book format. They are only eligible for paperback and hardcopy.

This is an issue for a few reasons;

- You are missing out on another income stream through e-books. There is a big market of Kindle readers that you can only target if you are a high content publisher.

- Not having an e-book version of your book means you cannot opt for kindle select when uploading your e-book, which puts you at a disadvantage to publishers who can.

One of the biggest advantages of having your book enrolled in kindle select is that you receive 5 days to promote your book for free every 90 days. Amazon will allow you to put your book in the Kindle store for free, allowing Kindle users to download your book for free.

This is especially helpful when you launch your book. As I mentioned in my previous book, the first 30 days of any book launch are crucial as they will be a huge determining factor in how Amazon's algorithm ranks your book when customers search for queries relevant to your book title.

When you put your book on a free book promo in the first 30 days of launch, whether that is 5 consecutive days or by breaking the days down how you see fit, it will put your book in a better position to have it ranking on the first page and make consistent sales for months and years to come. This is because the free book promo influences your book's BSR (the best seller's rank). That means that while you are not paid for putting your book in a free book promo, it will positively influence your book's ranking if you get a sizable number of downloads during the period.

This has really helped me rank new books on the first page of Amazon by leveraging the free book promo dates, which I would not have been able to do if I was a low/no content publisher.

Another reason the promo dates are very useful is that over time, I get more reviews for the book I promoted with the free book promo dates. This is from readers who downloaded the book during the free promo and may have left their review a few months later. These reviews will be very helpful as they serve as social proof and allow you to sell more books.

High content books tend to be ever-green, whereas low-content books are seasonal

An evergreen niche is a niche that sells all year round. It's a niche that does not rely on seasons, events, or holidays. An example of evergreen niches could be parenting, weight loss books, or books about relationships. These books will sell all year round, regardless of the time of year.

Whereas many low-content books are based on themes such as Halloween, Easter, or Christmas. That means that, yes, during those festive periods, the book sales are high, but that only lasts for a month or two during the entire year. That means that those books are completely dead during the other ten months.

Of course, this is not the case for all low-content books, but many of them are seasonal. So, even if you did want to get into low content, pick a niche and keyword that is not seasonable. One that will make you money all year round.

Low content books are restricted to only Amazon

While Amazon makes up the majority of high-content self-publishers' incomes, it's nice to know that they can diversify through audiobooks (audible), Ingramspark, D2D etc.

Low-content books are not only not allowed to be uploaded as e-books, but they also are frowned upon by platforms like Ingramspark (aggregator), Draft2digital, and Audible for audiobooks.

You are really shooting yourself in the foot by only publishing low-content books, in my opinion, as it is very hard for you to diversify your income and publish elsewhere outside of Amazon. If your account were, for whatever reason, to be closed by Amazon, you would certainly be screwed.

Take This Approach

If you are a beginner reading this, convinced about high content publishing but perhaps held back by your budget, here is what I would recommend:

You should start with low-content publishing. However, when I say that, I don't mean the same low-content books everyone else does. Your books should be different, higher quality, and focus on quality control. Once you start making a decent amount of money with low-content publishing, use that money to invest in your first writer for a high-content book.

Doing high content and low content at the same time is not a bad idea. You could publish a few low-content books while you wait for your high-content book to be written by your ghostwriter. There are many different ways you can approach it. Still, if I were starting over again with a tight budget, I would start with low content and eventually invest my profits into a high-content book. From there, you should continue re-investing the profits and building your portfolio even bigger.

Chapter 3: Why Self-Publishing Is The Best Online Opportunity For Beginners In 2023

Before I succeeded with self-publishing, I tried many different online business models.

This chapter will explain why self-publishing is the best business model to start in 2023. My views are not biased, as I do not have a course to sell you, so this does not benefit me. Alright then, let's compare the most well-known online business models today with self-publishing.

Why self-publishing is better than Affiliate Marketing

If you are not aware, affiliate marketing is when you sell another person's product, whether physical or digital, and you receive a commission from that sale. This is tracked through an 'Affiliate link', which tracks the sale of the product to you, the affiliate marketer.

While this seems very lucrative to the blind eye, it is actually not beginner friendly at all. Let me tell you why:

To succeed with affiliate marketing, you need an audience, whether through social media or by building an email list through your blog or even a YouTube channel. Building an audience takes months and sometimes even years.

Without an audience, your chances of success are very low. People without audiences who succeed with affiliate marketing spend heavily on paid advertising. As a beginner with a low budget, this is likely out of reach for you.

Whereas when self-publishing, you don't need to worry about driving traffic to your book, as your ideal customers are already shopping on Amazon, it is simply your job to drive traffic to your book listing, which you can do through low-cost per-click ads via Amazon ads. People think you need huge budgets to get started with Amazon ads, but you can get started with very little, as you can set your bids for keywords and adjust your daily budgets.

Many affiliate programs offer subpar commission rates. Some even as low as 2-3%. This means that to make any substantial income from affiliate marketing. You need to sell thousands of products every month, which is unrealistic for most average people. That said, there are digital products with affiliate programs offering a 50%+ commission rate. Still, the caveat is that you have to apply to be part of their affiliate program, and it is unlikely that they will accept you as a beginner with no track record or portfolio of selling anything.

On the other hand, with self-publishing, we earn 60% of all paperback sales (after printing fees) and 70% of e-book sales. The margins are much higher, so it is much easier to make a full-time income as a beginner.

Why self-publishing is better than 'Dropshipping' or e-commerce

Dropshipping is a business model that became popular from 2016-2017. The idea with Dropshipping is to sell physical products you don't have inventory for. You would list a bunch of products on your website. Whenever you get an order, you use the customer's money to purchase the product from a website like AliExpress or Alibaba for a much cheaper price and pocket the difference. The idea is simple, yet I believe this business model has some major flaws. Let's discuss the following:

Finding a winning product can take months and thousands of dollars in ad spend

While it is nice to be able to sell products that you don't have in your possession, getting to a stage where you have a winning product that sells regularly is a tough task. This is because you have to be willing to spend thousands of dollars in ad spend on platforms like Facebook, google and YouTube. You have to be patient as you have to try multiple creatives and texts, and more often than not, you will find yourself running through a few thousand dollars before finding any luck with Dropshipping. This is cost inefficient for a beginner with a tight budget.

Whereas with self-publishing, you don't need thousands to get started. You can write your own book, or if you don't have the capacity to write your own book, you can get your book written and published for a few hundred bucks.

Also, while nothing is guaranteed in business, you are more likely to make money quicker with a high-quality niche, book, and cover compared to Dropshipping.

You are solely responsible for customer service

As the Dropshipper, you are liable for any customer complaints, delays in delivery, or lost parcels/packages. Anyone who has done any form of business knows how tough customer service can be, especially for online orders. From my personal experience and speaking to veteran Dropshippers, chargebacks and returns are often much higher than desired, leaving Dropshippers with tiny profit margins and many headaches and stresses.

On the other hand, self-publishing on Amazon is one of the most hand-off online business models. This is because KDP is a print-on-demand service, meaning that Amazon will only print your book and send it to a customer when you make a sale. On top of that, Amazon deals with customer service and returns, allowing you to focus solely on producing the best quality books for your readers. That sounds lucrative to me.

Why self-publishing is better than SMMA (Social media marketing agency)

Running your own marketing agency is one of the better online business models today, as it does not involve many of the flaws that I have mentioned for the previous two business models, and it can be started with virtually $0. Although, I still think that self-publishing is better and that the agency model still has some flaws. The idea with a social media marketing agency is that you find clients and sell them on a social media service like paid ads, content creation, SEO, etc. Let's discuss some of the issues with this business model.

You have to be a professional in the services you are offering

It's all good to offer paid ad services, SEO, or content creation/ video editing services, but you would first need to learn these skills yourself to a high level. As a beginner with no experience, this can take months and sometimes even years, depending on your situation. Sure, you could arbitrage your service offering, meaning that you sell the client your services, and you pay someone in a country with cheaper labor to deliver it for half the price and pocket the rest. This is not sustainable, and ultimately you are still a novice in your own business, as you don't understand the ins and outs of your offering.

In self-publishing, though, being a good writer or an expert in a field is desirable but not necessary.

Virtually all tasks in the self-publishing process can be outsourced, making this business model the most beginner friendly.

However, Let's say that you didn't have the funds to outsource the tiresome tasks of self-publishing. Still, these tasks are minor and can be learned quickly, like writing a 200-word book description, formatting a book in Microsoft Word, or designing a basic book cover on Canva. Just about anybody can learn these simple skills and make a killing on Amazon.

The churn rate of clients is often times high

The churn rate is when a client/business stops doing business with you. I have spoken to many agency owners who always complain about high churn rates. But why do clients churn if you are providing a great service? This is what a person would think from the outside looking in, but a lot of the time, the service provided by the agency could be better, and therefore the clients leave after 3 or 4 months. This puts the agency owner back at stage 1, where they must cold call and email hundreds of prospects to find new clients. It's a vicious stressful cycle if you ask me. However, Let's say that you provide excellent services and have a low churn rate as an agency. Still, do you want clients constantly breathing at your doorstep, asking about the progress of your work? I wouldn't want that.

In self-publishing, there is no client. The clients are your readers. Your job is to produce a great quality book (discussed in detail in my first book) that your readers would enjoy reading. Let's say you don't produce a high-quality book, which reflects in your lack of book sales. In this case, you are not responsible to a client or boss.

That book will still generate some small monthly income, and you immediately move on to the next one.

Self-publishing is the most stress-free and predictable online business model that one can start. You control your destiny in self-publishing, as you have full authority over quality control. Unfortunately, this is not the case with an agency, as a client could still leave you regardless of how great your services are (for multiple reasons).

My conclusion

These are the three most popular online business models people love to discuss in 2023. Of course, there are more online opportunities. However, I did not want to make this chapter longer. I hope you get the idea.

Self-publishing is accessible to anyone, regardless of age, occupation, or circumstance. The tasks in the self-publishing process are easily outsourceable, but even if you want to learn them yourself, they are easy to learn and have little of a learning curve.

Chapter 4: Why Your Books Are Not Selling

This is a common thing I see from the dozen Facebook groups and communities I am part of; many people actively publish books but have yet to see the fruits of their labor so far. In this chapter, we will discuss the six main things you need to do better that are holding you back from achieving your royalty goals.

Your book SUCKS! Nobody wants to read it

Many publishers think their book is destined for success as long as they find a profitable niche with low competition and high demand. No, finding a profitable keyword is only the first stage.

We sometimes need to be more aware or realize that there is actually a final reader on the other side of our work. Readers who are not shy to share their thoughts about your book. They paid for it, after all, so they should be entitled to their opinion.

I have observed that many self-publishers rush the book creation process because they think they have found a diamond of a keyword and want to be the first in that niche to become an authority figure. This often leads to sloppy work that doesn't solve any problems for readers and often leaves them disappointed.

One of the main reasons your book is not selling is that it SUCKS, and you don't want to admit it.

Be honest with yourself. Have you spent time proofreading your work multiple times? Were you creative with your book title? Is your book description attractive to buyers and makes them want to know more?

For you to be successful with a book, the following four factors all need to be intact:

- An attractive book cover that sets you apart
- A creative book title and subtitle
- A well-written book description
- Your book actually needs to be good!

A publisher could have a great cover, a creative title and subtitle, and a really enticing book description but if your book is not as great as it may appear from the outside, it will not sell. Bad reviews will catch up with you sooner than you think, and your book sales will be completely dead before you know it.

If you want a full guide on how to write a great book, then please check out my previous book, 'How to successfully self-publish a book on Amazon & Audible' as I include a step-by-step breakdown in that book from finding profitable keywords, coming up with the contents of your book and structure and many more important topics regarding the writing of your book.

Your book is not formatted properly

Unfortunately, many self-publishers look over the formatting of the manuscript. Don't get it wrong. I am not saying you need to spend hundreds of dollars to get a perfectly formatted manuscript, but it should be at least formatted correctly.

Potential readers can read a sample of your book on the book listing (5-10% of the book), giving them a good idea of how the book will look once printed on paper. If they don't like the formatting of your book, even if it is the greatest book in the world, they will not purchase it.

It's something that skips a lot of self-publishers' minds as they often want to publish as many books as possible as quickly as possible. Remember, this is a book, not a college or university assignment! I have seen many books that look promising, but the books do not hit their potential due to the poor formatting.

I usually don't spend more than $40 to have my whole manuscript professionally formatted. You can find many freelancers to do this for you on Upwork or Fiverr. The most important thing here is to pay attention to book formatting, as it is very important.

Your keyword is too broad – you need to niche down!

What do I mean by this? Let me give you a real example.

Let's say you did your keyword research with KDspy (more on this in my first book) and concluded that the keyword 'Investing for beginners' was profitable. What most people would do at this stage is to go and hire a ghostwriter to write a book about investing for beginners.

The problem is that the keyword 'Investing for beginners' is too broad.

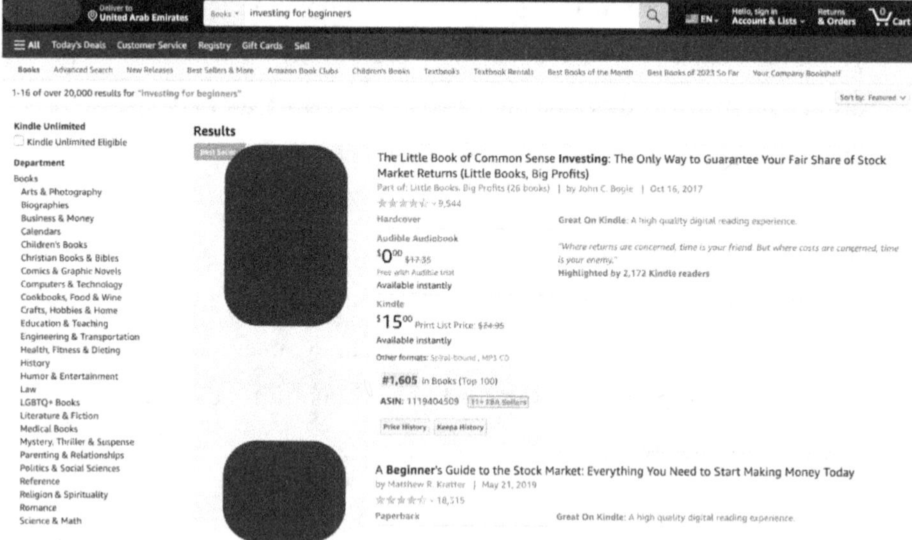

As you can see from the screenshot above, that claim is backed up by the sheer number of search results for the keyword 'Investing for beginners' (20,000 +)

Of course, you will struggle to sell your book if the keyword is too broad like this. Books that are too broad are a problem because they don't have an actual target audience, nor do they solve an actual problem. Rather they attempt to solve multiple problems in one manuscript, which is not a good idea for multiple reasons:

1. It is unrealistic for you to be a master/expert in all fields of investing (or whatever your book topic is on).

2. It shows a lack of credibility.

Instead, what a person should aim to do is really niche down. Let's continue with the same keyword, 'Investing for Beginners.' Let me show you how I would niche down this keyword to find that passionate group of readers who would purchase my book.

The first step is to choose what **type** of investing you want to target. This could be:

- Real estate investing
- Crypto Investing
- Stock market investing
- Bonds Investing
- Mutual funds investing
- Any other form of investing

For the sake of this example, let's say I want to go with 'Real estate investing for beginners.'

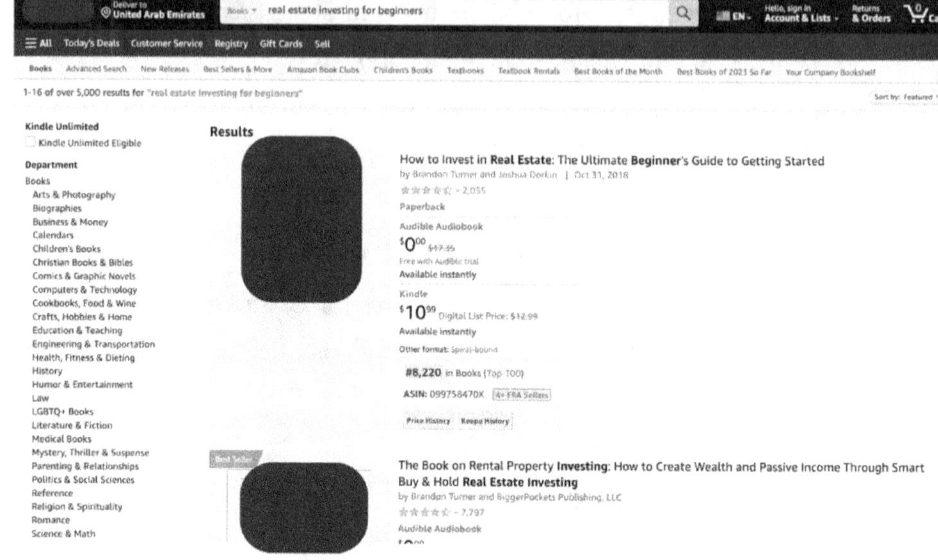

As you can see, 'Real estate investing for beginners' has over 5,000 search results, which is too much competition in most cases.

Okay, so the next step is to niche down even more!

Let's say I wanted to target women, so the keyword would now become 'Real estate investing for women.'

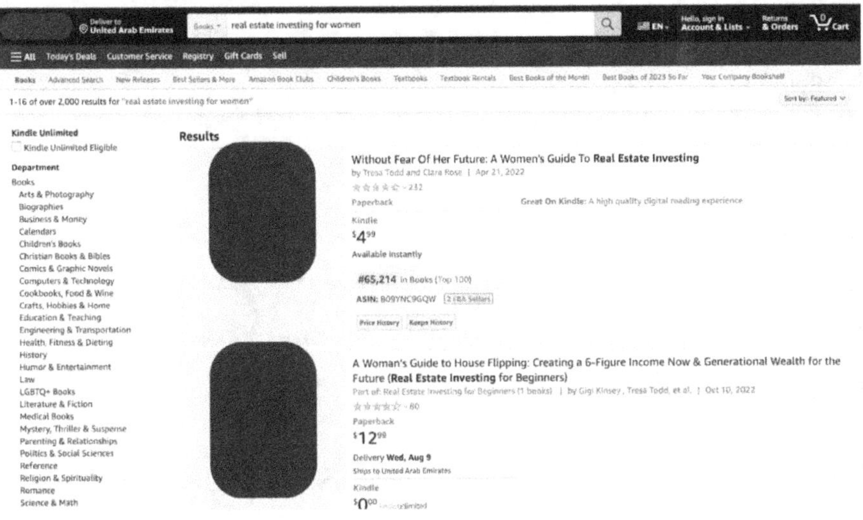

As you can see now from the search results, the competition is way less! This is what you need to do. Of course, you need to ensure the keyword is profitable (using KDspy). Niching down like this will help you to sell your books as it will show customers that you have a very specific target market for your book, and that is fine! Authors and self-publishers must understand that their book is not for everyone, which is totally okay!

Let me give you another two examples.

Let's say, at first glance, the keyword 'Coding for beginners' appeared to be a profitable keyword. Again, what most people would do from this stage is to create a book on coding while filling the book with multiple coding languages and concepts.

Instead, I would **niche down** further.

The first thing I would look at is the different types of coding languages. They could be, for example:

- Python

- JavaScript

- SQL

- HTML

- C++

From here, I will take it further and try to niche down again.

For example, I might go for something like 'JavaScript programming for teens.'

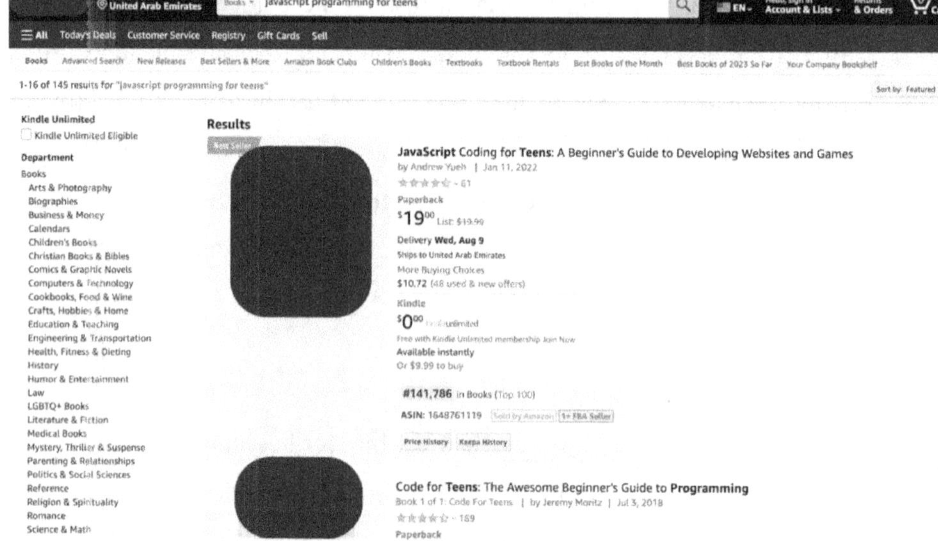

As you can see now, the keyword has way fewer search results. Another benefit to doing it this way is that if you tackle one very niche keyword to a high level, you will build an audience of readers who love and trust your work. From there, you can create a series of books and build more credibility.

It's harder to build credibility when you are too broad in your keywords, as you are not solving a real problem for a specific group of people but instead trying to solve everyone's problems, which is never ideal or realistic. Of course, when you use this method, make sure that the keyword is profitable by following the metrics that I mentioned in my first book, 'How To Successfully Self-Publish A Book On Amazon And Audible.'

Let me give you the last example.

Let's say I went with the keyword 'Keto diet for beginners.'

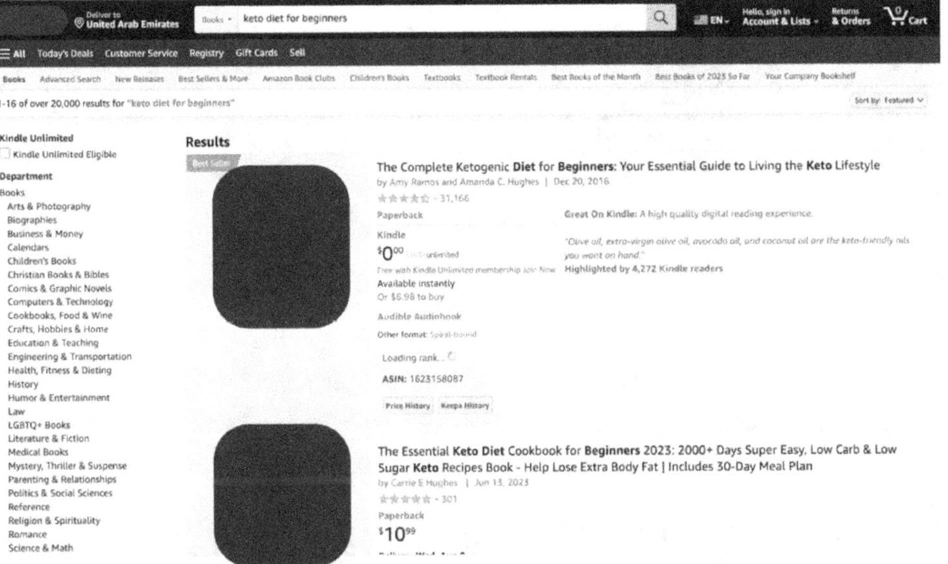

As you can see, the keyword presents more than 20,000 search results, which is too much competition!

The next thing I would do from here is to **niche down** again.

Let's say I niched down to 'Keto diet for women'. This is okay, but I want to narrow it down further to 'Keto diet for women over 60.'

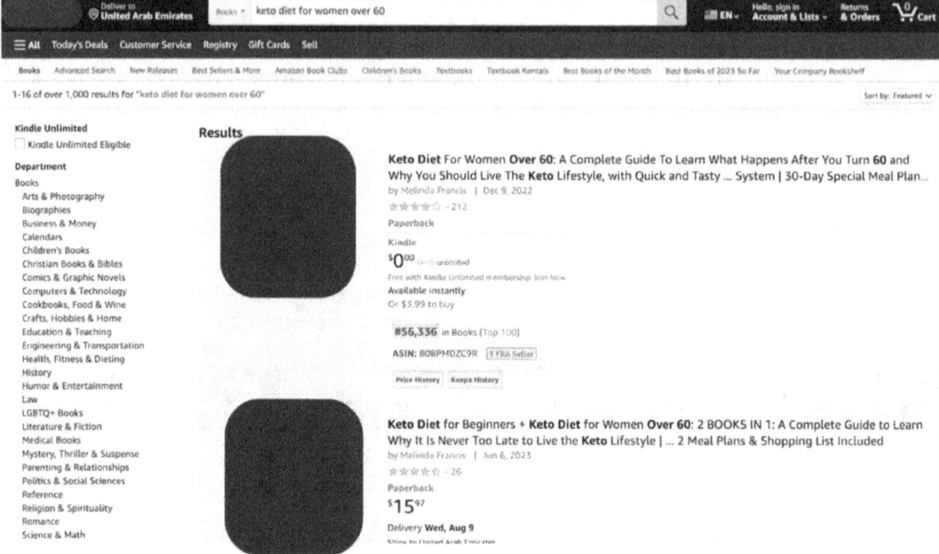

As you can see, the search results are again a lot less, meaning fewer people are competing with you. You can focus on creating a high-quality book that solves the problem of this specific target audience of women over the age of 60.

Your pricing strategy is ineffective

This is a huge one. One that publishers often really overlook.

We have to remember that there are real customers on the other side who are purchasing our books. We have to price our books strategically. What do I mean by that?

The price of your e-book/paperback/hardback needs to be within the range of your competition. That means that you should not **<u>undercut</u>** your competitors and price your book too low, and not **<u>overprice</u>** your book to where it becomes too expensive and unaffordable for customers.

Let me give you an actual example.

Let's say the top 5 competitors on the first page of my niche price their paperbacks at:

1. $12.99
2. $13.50
3. $11.99
4. $13.25
5. $13.99

It is common to see these sorts of prices on the first page of a search query (for high content publishing). I think pricing my book 'competitively' in a scenario like this would result in a paperback price of $12.75 – or something along those lines. This is because the book is not the cheapest out of the competition but not the most expensive; it's that nice sweet spot in the middle.

Pricing your book too low in this scenario would be a price such as $9.99. This is because:

1) customers could get the impression that you are not an actual 'expert' in your field/niche, and for that reason, they could avoid your book, and 2) it would likely also hurt your competition as readers would constantly double think purchasing a book more than $9.99. ultimately, everybody loses in this scenario, which is not what we want!

With that said, during the first 30 days of any book launch, you need to reduce the price of your book purposely. I usually do it by 25%. If I were to usually price my book at $12.99, I would price my book at $9.99 during the first 30 days.

As I have explained in my first book, Amazon's algorithm gives every new book a slight boost over its competition, meaning that they may rank your book higher than your competitors for that period and give it more exposure. Why do they do this, though?

Amazon does this because they want to test the waters with your book. If your book sells hundreds of copies in the first month, that is a good indication to Amazon's algorithm to rank it on the first page, as that is what customers buy for that search query. However, if you get few sales during your book launch, Amazon will likely rank your book on your keyword's 9th or 10th page. Your book will be inaccessible to your target market, making you the loser as you would miss out on a TON of organic traffic and sales.

This brings me to my next point very nicely, which is:

<u>Self-publishers neglect the launch</u>

A successful book launch is the most important determining factor in whether your book will be a hit or miss in the long term. As I have already mentioned, the first 30 days are crucial, and it should be your goal as a self-publisher to sell as many e-books/paperback/hard copies of your book during this period.

Most beginners need to realize that the **REAL** money made from self-publishing is not from your ads. Rather it is the organic sales that you get from your book. Most self-publishers are not actually directly profitable from their Amazon ads. Rather, the ads are a crucial driving factor in ranking your book, which is where the money is made in the long run.

In that case, why should I run ads then?

That's a fair question/thought to have. I'll tell you why.

Running ads, especially straight from launch, is crucial as they will dramatically help you get those sales you desperately need in the first 30 days. Most self-publishers do not take the launch seriously and do not launch their ads until they get 5-10 reviews on their book. I think this is wrong because you are wasting the 30-day grace period that Amazon gives you during the launch.

Most self-publishers fear losing money during the first 30 days of launch and try to play it safe. But if you ask the professionals, they will tell you that the first 30 days are NOT about making a profit on your book.

Myself, I will often lose money or break even during the first month of launch because my aim is not to profit during the first month, I aim to get as many book sales as possible and rank my book, and that means being as aggressive as I can with Amazon ads.

I am not saying you need to spend thousands of dollars on Amazon ads in the first month of launch. Spend within your means. However, you should not be hesitant to invest in ads during this period, as it will ultimately pay off in the long run.

When a book is launched successfully, and you have it ranking on the first page of your keyword after the 30-day incubation period, what will happen is your book will be high in the search results. Thanks to Amazon's algorithm, your book will get a TON of organic traffic. This organic traffic will more often than not lead to a TON of organic sales (provided that your book is good, of course) and will continue to snowball for months and years.

Whereas compare this to somebody who neglected their launch, was too scared to invest some money into ads, and the books ultimately stopped selling after a few months. It sounds really easy, right? Yet beginners need to understand the importance of Amazon ads and the purpose they serve. Even if you are unprofitable from the ads, if you launch your book properly, the organic sales should make that up and make you profitable.

The aim should not be to become profitable with your book in the first month, rather self-publishing is a long-term game. If you follow this strategy and do everything as you should, I can guarantee that in a year, you will be super glad that you did, as it will ultimately lead to success.

<u>You are neglecting A+ Content</u>

A+ content was introduced to Amazon in 2016. It allows authors to add images, comparison tables, and texts to your product page. This is done to engage readers while also informing them more about your book, perhaps some information that you could not fit in your book description.

According to a study conducted by Amazon, they monitored 100,000 ASINs over a 90-day time period and concluded that books with basic A+ content resulted in an average increase in book sales by 5.6%.

This statistically proves that you are more likely to succeed with your book if you have A+ content. With that said, I see many people do A+ content wrong. When you are creating your A+ content, take the following into account:

1. You need to show the core selling points of your book in a visually appealing way. I always invest in graphic designers to create me visually appealing graphics.

2. Look at what the best-selling books in your niche are doing with their A+ content. Don't copy it, but add your own twist to it. They may be missing out on something you can include in your A+ content.

3. Don't fill your A+ content with too much text! You don't want to overwhelm your customers with too much text; you should focus more on the visual appeal.

4. Optimize your A+ content for mobile devices. Unfortunately, many self-publishers miss out on this crucial task, and their A+ content that looks decent on a computer/laptop may look out of sync on a mobile device. You need to specifically optimize the A+ content for your mobile device.

These are the main reasons that people often don't see success with self-publishing. Of course, there are many other small reasons. If you get the above six correct, it is very hard not to succeed with self-publishing, provided that you have a high-quality book that is in demand.

Chapter 5: Updates To The Amazon Algorithm 2023

The Amazon algorithm has significantly changed from when I started publishing in late 2019 to now (2023). A lot of things have changed. Some would say for the better, and others would argue for the worst. In this chapter, I will explain the differences and how you can use them to your advantage.

The OLD algorithm

A few years ago, Amazon ranked books based on **SEO** (Search engine optimization).

If your book contained certain keywords in your metadata (your title, subtitle, and the 7 back-end keywords when uploading your book to KDP), it would show up to that target market, even if your book had nothing to do with those keywords.

This was problematic because it led to many self-publishers who tried to game the system by keyword stuffing.

Keyword stuffing is trying to stuff in as many keywords in your title as possible, regardless of whether they are relevant to your book.

Let me give you an example.

Back in the day, someone's main keyword might have been 'How To Analyze People,' in their title, they may have proceeded to include keywords like; dark psychology, gaslighting, emotional intelligence, and more irrelevant keywords.

Why would someone do this, you may ask?

It's simple, the algorithm at that time could not differentiate whether your book fell into those categories or not, meaning that if someone searched the terms' 'Dark Psychology' or 'Gaslighting' the book that was intended for 'How To Analyze People' may have showed up only because you included those additional keywords in your title, even though they have nothing to do with your book.

Amazon later realized that this algorithm needed to be changed as people were stuffing a ton of keywords into their book titles to game the system and get more organic traffic to their books. Another reason why Amazon addressed this issue is that it was giving customers a poor shopping experience. If you know anything about Amazon, you know that customer experience is at the heart of their platform.

The NEW algorithm

Thanks to the development of technology in the last few years, Amazon has significantly improved its algorithm and made it a fair playing field for everybody.

Let me tell you why.

Now, Amazon does not actually rank your book based on the keywords in your title or subtitle. Rather, your book is ranked based on where the sales are coming from.

Let me give you an example.

If your keyword was 'Self-regulation workbook for kids.'

Yes, your book may still be ranking for that keyword. However, you may also find your book ranking for keywords such as 'CBT activities for kids' or 'Emotional regulation activities for kids'; this is because the Amazon algorithm may detect that many of your sales are coming from people with these search queries.

Also, as Amazon's algorithm has now become so smart, another way that it now ranks our books is by simply guessing what our books are about based on the metadata (The title, subtitle, 7 keywords in the back end), EVEN if the main keyword is not used in the title.

This, in my opinion, is great, as it not only weaves out the people who were trying to make a quick buck by gaming the algorithm, but it also allows authors and self-publishers to be more creative with their titles and subtitles without worrying that their main keyword is not in there. This now means that you will not find poor-quality books ranking on the first and second page of a search query, which is great! It gives self-publishers like you and me an opportunity to produce a high-quality book that serves our readers. The algorithm now is a lot more rewarding for serious self-publishers.

We are at a time where machine learning is improving as technology improves. Big companies like Amazon will continue to update and change their algorithm. In my opinion, it is better as it gives indie authors and non-fiction self-publishers more opportunity to rank their books and make a ton of money, regardless of how popular their author's name is. This will lead to higher-quality books being published, which is surely a win-win for everyone.

Chapter 6: Amazon Ads – Why Most People Can't Make Them Work

In this chapter, I will break down the importance of Amazon ads and explain the most common reasons why people cannot make them work in the long term. This chapter will not include a step-by-step guide on how to set up Amazon ads, as I have already done that in my previous book, 'How to successfully Self-publish a Book on Amazon and Audible.'

It Is Not All About Your 'ACOS'

Remember how I said that 'ACOS' (advertising cost of sales) is not the be-all and end-all metric for Amazon ads. I want to demonstrate that with the below screenshot from one of my campaigns.

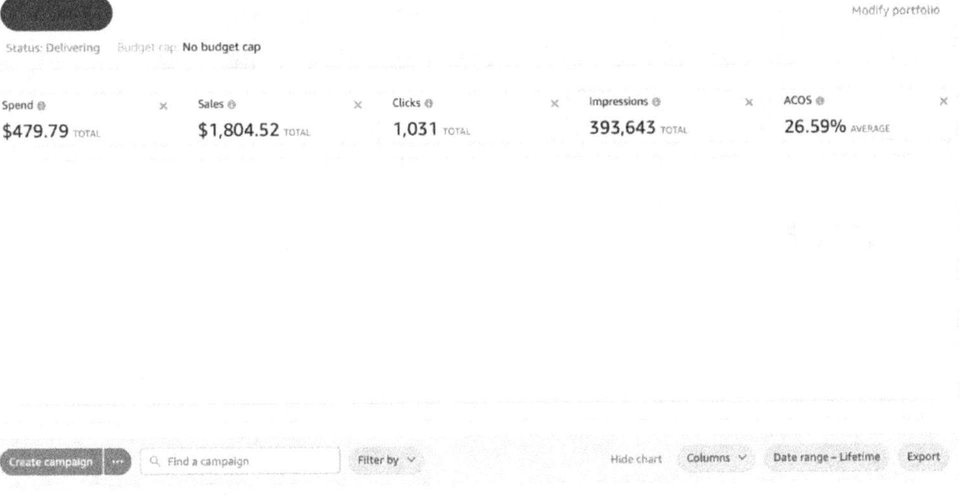

This is the lifetime Amazon ads dashboard for one of my books. At first glance, a beginner may think that this campaign is not profitable solely based on the ACOS, which is 26% here. This is because a lot of gurus will tell you that you should aim for an ACOS that is between 10-20%, which by the way, is really hard to achieve. I'm here to tell you that ACOS should not be the only metric that you consider when it comes to deciding whether or not to switch off your campaign. Let me tell you why.

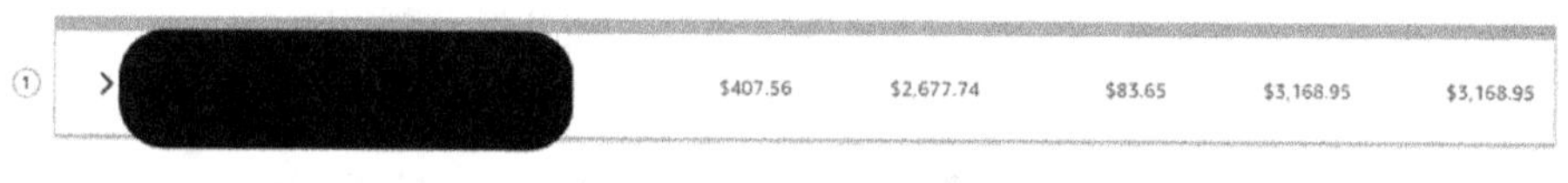

These are the lifetime royalties that I received from this same book. Now, if we look at the amount I spent on ads ($480) compared to the lifetime royalties that I took home ($3,168), we can see that there is actually a very healthy profit margin here, regardless of the slightly higher ACOS at 26%. This is why I said that Amazon ads are only there to drive organic traffic to your book. Your aim should NOT be to become profitable from ads.

Let me give you another example.

This is another book that I launched late last year. Since launching this book, you can see I have spent about $460 on ads for this book. Again, at first sight, you may think that the ACOS (29%) is really high here and that I should switch off the campaign.

Again, if we look at the lifetime royalties for this book, it by war outweighs the amount I have spent on ads for it, making it a very profitable book for me.

This also links to the other point I mentioned about switching off your ads too early. When you first launch your book, especially during the first month, you must understand that you will likely take a loss during this period. The first month is all about trial and error, seeing which keywords convert and which do not. But you cannot get to that stage if you switch off your Amazon ads too early because you are concerned about the ACOS.

I get it... it's not nice seeing your money being eaten up by advertising costs and seeing very little in return during that period. Still, if you are really serious about self-publishing, then it is something that you have to come to terms with, as self-publishing is a long-term game.

You need to use the first month as a trial-and-error month and pull out some extra cash you would be willing to lose. Once you have enough data, you can make more calculated decisions regarding switching off campaigns or keeping them running, but it's hard to do that when you constantly switch off campaigns.

Lastly, this also explains why keyword research is SUPER important. If you pick a keyword that is not profitable or one that is too competitive, regardless if you are patient with your ads or not, it will probably not work out for you in the long term, as it is really hard to rank a book that has a lot of competition with hundreds if not thousands of reviews on the first page, and it is also hard to make consistent sales in a nice that doesn't have enough demand. There needs to be the right balance there. The keyword should be profitable and also not have too much competition. Also, remember what I said about niching down your keyword, as that is really important if you want to succeed.

Should you target your e-book/hardback copy?

In my personal experience, I have tried to run ads with e-books, but it has not been as successful for me compared to paperback copies. You also have to remember that with e-books, it's a lot easier for customers to return the book and get their money back, and unfortunately, this is a thing that happens.

Another reason I prefer to solely run ads for paperbacks is that the royalty rate I get for paperbacks is much more. For me personally, I like to earn a minimum of $5 per sale after Amazon's fees and printing costs. Unfortunately, it is hard to do that with e-books as the delivery fee with e-books is usually really high. You would have to raise the price of your e-book by a lot to get a royalty rate of $5.

Now this can be tricky because, if you remember, I said that you should base the prices of your books and e-books based on your competition.

If your competition has their e-books listed at $1.99 and $2.99, it won't make sense for you to charge $8.99 for your e-book because customers would likely not purchase them. For this reason, I solely run ads on my paperback as I have more flexibility with the margins.

In terms of hardback copies, I have realized that the costs for them are ridiculously high, and the royalty rate for them is really low.

For example, a paperback book with 105 pages and a list price of $12.99 has a royalty rate of $5.64 per sale, which is healthy.

However, a hardcopy book with 105 pages and a list price of $12.99 has a royalty rate of $0.99, which is really low!

To make any money from hard copies, you would have to list your book at a really high price. Therefore, I also don't run ads on hardback copies of my books as nobody would spend that much on my book. It is a good idea, though, to publish them anyway and leave them there, as you may make a few organic sales on them from time to time, which is nice!

Should you take Amazon's 'Recommended bid' price seriously?

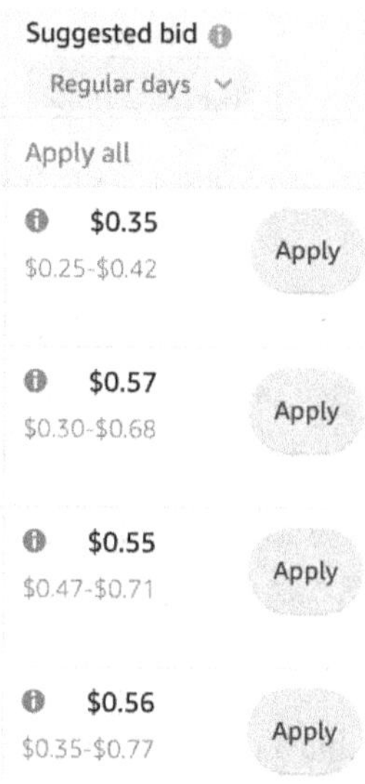

When you enter target words in your campaign, you will often see a 'suggested bid' price for target words that you enter. A lot of people take this very seriously and end up going with the suggested bid from Amazon.

Based on my experience, the suggested bids can be really off. For example, Amazon may recommend you to bid $0.50 per click for that target word, but you can actually get that same click for $0.25-$0.30.

As I have explained in my previous book, Amazon works on a bidding system, but just because you bid higher for a target word than your competition, it doesn't mean that your book will be given priority. Books of the highest quality that have the most consistent sales will often win the bid.

This means that I can bid $0.50 for a target word, my competitor can bid $0.25, and he can win it over me.

For this reason, to avoid wasting money on clicks, it's always a good idea to start low with your bids and slowly raise them. Suppose you see that you are not getting the impressions that you wanted, in that case you should gradually raise the bid. However, you should NOT start bidding highly, like $0.50+, as it could lead to you wasting a lot of money with ads that could have been avoided.

Chapter 7: Consider Going Wide (Ingramspark)

If you've been a self-publisher/author for a while, you probably know what 'going wide' means. If you have not, I will explain in this chapter why I believe it is a good idea to go wide as a self-published author.

'Going Wide'

When someone says 'Going wide' in self-publishing, they mean spreading your wings with where your books are published.

While Amazon is the largest online bookstore, there are also other places where you can publish your book and make additional income, although what I will definitely say is that the bulk of your income will come from Amazon (70%+). Some of the most popular alternatives to Amazon, where people will publish their books, are platforms like Ingramspark, Google Books, Draft2digital, and Kobo Books.

Many of these platforms are simply global distribution networks that will distribute your books to other online bookstores besides Amazon. Some platforms will also distribute your book to retailers like Walmart, Barnes and Noble, Target and many schools and libraries, which is super cool! Imagine shopping at Walmart and seeing your book on the bookshelf? That must be a great feeling.

The rules for e-books

There is an important rule you need to be aware of if you wish to distribute your e-book with other platforms outside of Amazon.

Your e-book mustn't be enrolled into KDP Select.

When you upload your e-book on Amazon KDP, on the last page, it will ask you if you wish to enrol your book into KDP Select. What does this mean?

What is 'KDP select?'

The KDP Select program allows authors and self-publishers to benefit financially and gain promotional rewards from Amazon.

When you enrol your book into KDP Select, one of the rules that Amazon state is that you must only publish your e-book exclusively with them. Which means that you can't 'go wide'. If you don't follow this rule, you could get in serious trouble and potentially lose your account.

Another important thing to mention is that books enrolled in KDP Select are freely available for customers who are subscribed to Amazon's Kindle Unlimited program.

Kindle Unlimited is a program set up by Amazon.

The idea is that customers pay a $9.99 fee per month, giving them access to as many Kindle Unlimited e-books as they'd like per month. However, customers can only have 10 Kindle unlimited books in their Kindle at a time. Of course, they can return books and pick up others, but this number cannot exceed 10. 'KDP Select' is basically the back end of Kindle Unlimited. This means that if you enrol your book into KDP Select, Kindle Unlimited users can read your book freely.

This probably sounds horrible, right? Well, there are actually some great benefits to this.

As I said above, financial benefits exist for the author who enrols their e-book into the KDP select program. Enrolled books into KDP Select are eligible for $0.00412 per page read by Kindle Unlimited users. While that is a little amount, based on my experience, it can add up at the end of the month and be another nice source of income, especially if you already have a few good books out.

What are the promotional benefits of being enrolled in KDP select? Amazon gives KDP select authors a 5-day free book promotion every 90-day period. This means you can offer your book for free for 5 days in total (for both kindle unlimited users and non-kindle unlimited users). Why is this a benefit, you may ask?

When you schedule your book for a free book promo, yes, people will be able to download it for free, and you are not paid for that. However, it gives your book a lot of exposure and helps with your book ranking.

I have had a book have over 2000 downloads in 1 day, and it spiked my book up in the search engines and really increased my royalties. Also, if you are an indie author or a brand-new self-publisher just getting started, you likely won't have a big audience of fans or people who enjoy your books. I think you have nothing to lose here and a lot to gain. I enrol all of my books into kindle select, and I think it is definitely worth it.

Another promotional benefit of enrolling in KDP Select is that you are eligible for Kindle countdown deals. What are they, you may be asking?

Kindle countdown deals allow authors to run discounts on their e-books for a limited time. This only applies to Amazon.com and Amazon.co.uk. I have also used this, and I love it for a few reasons:

- When customers see time-based discounts on your e-book, it creates scarcity and excitement. Also, when you run the countdown deal, it shows both the original and discounted list price, meaning that customers can see the great deal they are getting.

- You still earn the same 70% royalty rate for your e-book! – this is really cool! This means that as long as your book is not priced higher than $9.99, you will still receive the same 70% royalty rate on your discounted list price that you would have received at the original price.

- You can also monitor the performance of the countdown deal in real-time. Why not try it? And if it doesn't work, you don't have to do it again.

With all of this said, some people still prefer not to have their books enrolled in the KDP Select program for various reasons, although I think the mean reason is that they may have previously tried it with another book, and it did not go as planned. Therefore, they want to spread their wings and publish their books on other platforms.

Personally, though, I would definitely recommend authors to enrol their e-book in the KDP select program as I believe the benefits by far outweigh any negatives. However, if you are a more established author with a large fan base, it is probably better not to enrol your book into KDP Select, as customers would pay for your e-book anyway.

So just to round up, if your e-book is enrolled in KDP Select, you cannot publish your book outside of Amazon. You are exclusive to Amazon. Although I also like that you can remove your book from the KDP Select program at any time. If you are unhappy and wish to distribute your books outside of KDP, you can simply contact Amazon and ask them to remove your book from the program. Please wait for their confirmation to say that your book was successfully removed from the program before going and uploading it to other websites.

What about paperback copies? Are there any rules for them?

When it comes to paperback/hardback copies of your book, it becomes a lot easier. This is because KDP select only applies to e-books, not paperbacks or hardback copies.

'Expanded distribution' – should you go for it or not?

| | Amazon ⌄ | | | Expanded Distribution ⌄ | |
Printing ⌄	Rate ⌄	Royalty ⌄		Rate ⌄	Royalty ⌄
$2.48	60%	$6.51	☐	40%	$3.51

When uploading your paperback version of your book, you will be asked how you would like to distribute your book. Whether through Amazon (the standard option) or what is known as 'Expanded distribution'. The question is, what is expanded distribution?

Expanded distribution essentially is a partnership that Amazon has with Ingramspark, where Amazon distributes paperback books to libraries, bookstores, online retailers, and others on your behalf across a number of territories across the world. As the name suggests, you are expanding the distribution of your book, which may look enticing at first, but I don't recommend you do this.

Let me tell you why.

Before I talk about Ingramspark, it is important to mention that you cannot select 'expanded distribution' while also intending to publish your paperback book outside of Amazon, as it may lead to duplicates.

Therefore, if you wish to go for Ingramspark (which I recommend), please ensure that the 'expanded distribution' box is not ticked.

<u>**Ingramspark**</u>

As I have already mentioned earlier, Ingramspark is not the one who will sell your book. Rather they are only the distributors. How it works is that the retailers will order copies of your book through the Ingramspark distribution channel. After that, Ingramspark will print physical copies when they are ordered (it's a POD service) and ship them to their distribution partners, whether that is libraries or retailers.

Ingramspark claims to have a distribution network of 40,000+, which, to be honest, is hard to believe, although I do think that they have a great reach that you should not miss out on.

Recently, there was a major pricing change on Ingramspark. Until a few weeks ago, there was a $50 fee per book submission to Ingramspark. This was in place for a few years. It was by no means cheap, but in my opinion, it was worth it. Now, however, they have made it completely free. There are no more set-up fees. The only thing that you will still have to cover yourself is the ISBN for your book, which cannot be the same free ISBN from Amazon KDP. Although ISBNS are affordable when purchased in bulk.

If you asked me before the pricing change if I thought it was worth it to upload your books onto Ingramspark, I would have said yes. Now though, I think you would be silly not to upload your books to Ingramspark.

Since I started uploading my already available books on Amazon on Ingramspark about a year and a half ago as an additional income stream, I have made well over $3000 profit from it. The best part about this income stream is that it's literally set and forget. There are no ads on Ingramspark. There is no maintenance like with Amazon ads. You upload your books and collect passive income. You don't need to worry about anything!

Other distributors

You could use D2D, Lulu, or Barnes and Noble. Although my recommendation for paperbacks is to go solely with Ingramspark, as they have the largest distribution network and will most likely be your 2nd largest stream of income from your books after Amazon. Also, your book would go through all the same channels as D2D, Lulu, and Barnes and Noble anyway.

Chapter 8: Awesome New Platform For Book & Audiobook Reviews

Getting reviews for your books is one of those topics that I see discussed often. After all, reviews are very important as they serve as social proof and dramatically increase your conversion rates.

Unfortunately, some self-publishers illegally acquire reviews, and go against Amazon's review policies. This may be through paying people to leave positive reviews, influencing people to leave positive reviews, or simply review swapping, which are all not allowed and frowned upon by Amazon.

In my last book, 'How To Successfully Self-Publish A Book On Amazon & Audible', I recommended a platform called 'Pubby' as I thought it was a great legal way to get reviews for authors.

There is a new platform that I believe only launched in the last month that I am now using. The platform is called 'Bookbite' (www.bookbite.co).

I canceled my Pubby subscription and now only use this new platform. Let me explain why.

This is not a promotion, nor am I doing this to my benefit. As you can see, there is no affiliate link for me. I am only promoting this new platform because I believe it is revolutionary for publishers. I only recommend what I personally use myself and would not promote anything that I don't believe in.

The idea with Bookbite and Pubby is similar yet very different.

UI/ Dashboard

In my opinion, the general dashboard and UI are no comparison. Bookbite is better in every aspect. Not only is it more pleasing for the eyes, but the system functions more coherently.

With Pubby, you pick up other authors' books from the library (completely anonymous) and leave a review within a specific time frame. However, after being subscribed to Pubby for more than 6 months, the model has one big flaw. In my experience with Pubby, because authors have the flexibility of picking out any book in the library and reviewing it, it would often lead to generic and spammy reviews as people were after the coins they would get for reviewing those books, and then using them to get reviews for their own books. However, with Bookbite, it is totally different.

Bookbite works on a request to review functionality. This means that they encourage readers to request to review books in niches and categories they are genuinely passionate about. Readers would answer a series of four/five short questions that would be sent off to the author. The request is completely anonymous, making it compliant with Amazon's reviewing policy as the author does not know who the person is interested in reading their book.

The questions allow the author to understand if this prospect is a passionate fan of the niche, giving the author a good idea if the prospect will leave a high-quality review.

The author has 24 hours to respond to these anonymous requests from interested readers. They have the option to either accept or decline.

I have received higher-quality reviews from Bookbite than from Pubby

Bookbite is a brand-new platform, so it is still early days. However, the reviews I have received from Bookbite are of much higher quality than those from Pubby!

I used to get one-or two-line generic reviews from readers on Pubby. While many of those reviews were four and five stars, they didn't help me with my book sales as much as I'd thought they would. Let me explain why.

Amazon KDP is now becoming more mainstream and competitive, especially in the non-fiction space. The last time I checked, there were roughly around 7,500 new e-books being published on Amazon every day. That's crazy.

With more competition and books, that means that the average amount of reviews that you need for your books to pick up traction also increases. The problem now arises when everybody in your niche has 50-100+ reviews on their book.

Your competition may have mediocre one- or two-line reviews on their book, and in that case, the thing that will give your book an edge over theirs is most certainly the **quality** of reviews.

Customers are becoming much more wary with their money since the COVID-19 pandemic. A customer may have very convincingly purchased your book before the pandemic, although now, they are starting to double doubt every purchase, understandably so.

When you have high-quality reviews under your book that are constructive, helpful, and informative, it helps convince readers that are on the edge of purchasing your book. I am not saying that the reviews need to be paragraphs long, not at all. Although, a review should justify the rating given for the book. It should explain why the reader enjoyed or didn't enjoy it instead of a simple one-line review like 'Great book, loved it!' what did you love about the book?

Think about it. You're scrolling through Amazon looking for a new book to purchase. You come across two books. Book A and Book B. Book A has 40 high-quality, informative reviews that summarize the book's best parts. Book B has 70 low-quality reviews. A lot of reviews read like 'I enjoyed it' or 'Well written' or 'Great storyline'. Which book would you rather purchase? Which book would you have higher confidence in it being a hit?

I am not saying that one cannot get high-quality reviews from Pubby, although from my experience, most of the reviews are low-quality. Ultimately, Bookbite does not GUARANTEE you to get higher quality reviews than Pubby. However, I would say the owners have put the parameters in place for authors to sus out readers that will not do their book justice with the review.

You can get BOTH book & audiobook reviews on Bookbite

Pubby only caters to books, not audiobooks.

The platform costs $17.99 monthly to upload a maximum number of 10 books onto the platform and $29.99 monthly for an unlimited number of books. You can also subscribe to the annual unlimited package, which will set you back $240 annually.

Bookbite follows a similar pricing strategy, although the value for money is clear with Bookbite. Let me explain why.

With Bookbite, they offer three subscription packages. The first one is the 'Unlimited audiobook' package. This plan allows users to upload unlimited audiobooks to the platform. This is $19.99 a month. The 2nd plan is the 'Unlimited books' plan. Again, upload an unlimited number of books for $24.99 a month. The last plan, which is the most popular, is the 'Unlimited Books & Audiobooks' plan at $29.99 a month! This deal allows you to get unlimited reviews for both your books and audiobooks. This is a game-changer for me.

It is the same price as Pubby's subscription plan, but the value provided is a lot more as the platform also caters to audiobook publishers.

How it works on Bookbite is that the author would upload their ACX codes, and their audiobook would be listed in the 'Audiobook Library' from there. It's the same thing as books. Your request to review other people's audiobooks (anonymously).

Once a request is accepted, one of the ACX codes of the author is given to the listener. They will redeem the ACX code, listen to the audiobook and review it within a timeframe.

As a book publisher and audiobook publisher, I cannot stress enough how useful it is to get both book and audiobook reviews in the same place. Whenever I publish an audiobook, I need help to distribute the promotional codes that ACX gives me. Either people are not interested in the audiobook, but even if they are, they usually don't tend to leave a review on Audible. With Bookbite, people will listen to AND review your audiobook on audible. I know this will save me a lot of time trying to distribute codes online through Facebook and Reddit groups.

That's not all, though, there is one distinguishing feature that Bookbite has launched that I have not seen ANYWHERE else, and I absolutely love it!

You can get verified reviews on Bookbite WITHOUT you or your reader having to purchase any books!

I explained the difference between a verified review and an unverified review in my previous book 'How To Successfully Self-Publish A Book On Amazon & Audible.' Unverified reviews are inferior to verified reviews, as unverified reviews only show up in the marketplace that you leave them on. In contrast, verified reviews appear on ALL of the Amazon marketplaces and have the 'Verified Purchase' Tag. Verified reviews hold more value in the eyes of a customer.

How it works with Pubby is that you can get verified purchase reviews. However, you must list your e-book for a price in their library. Someone would then go and purchase your book and review it.

This still works, although It's, of course, cost-ineffective for reviewers because they have to purchase your e-book at full price. Which is often between $2.99 - $6.99 – this is pricey, especially if you do it a few times a month.

While Bookbite still offers the same option of buying and reviewing other people's books, they have introduced a new feature that allows authors to get verified reviews without reviewers having to purchase their books, which is fantastic! They are the first platform to offer this service.

They call it the 'Free Book Promo.' Your book must be enrolled into KDP Select (which 99% of us self-publishers already have), and the idea is that you place your book in a free book promo with KDP and you match the dates with Bookbite. Then your book would be displayed in the library for other readers to request. Once you approve a few readers, they will download your book on the promo dates that you stated and leave a review once they have finished reading it.

This will lead to a verified review because Amazon counts these downloads as 'Purchases', and they qualify for the verified purchase badge. However, one thing to note is that this is only applicable to reviewers who do not possess a kindle unlimited account. This is because if you leave a review for a book you downloaded during the promo if you have a kindle unlimited account, the review will not be verified as Amazon classes it as a 'borrow' rather than a 'purchase'.

I was unaware of this phenomenon, but it is a brilliant way for just about any author to get verified purchase reviews. This really is a game-changer!

Let me discuss the last thing I like about this new platform.

You can get reviews on ALL the Amazon marketplaces!

One thing I did not particularly enjoy about Pubby was that whenever I went for the standard review type, meaning that my reader would download my book and leave a review, I would never know which marketplace I would find my review on. Remember, standard unverified reviews do not show up on all Amazon marketplaces, only the one you left the review on. For example, if you left an unverified review on Amazon.es (Spanish Amazon), that review would be restricted to Amazon.es. It wouldn't transfer over to Amazon.com. This was a problem because I often found the review on a marketplace irrelevant to the one I sell most of my books in. Pubby would make it unclear as to where I would find the review. Sometimes it would be on the US site and sometimes on the UK, and I've even found a few reviews on Amazon.In (India).

What Bookbite has done is that they give authors a chance to select which Amazon marketplace they would like their book to be reviewed in if they go for the Kindle unlimited and free/standard reader types.

Then, when readers are in the library, they can filter out books by marketplace. So, for instance, if a reader wanted to find listings with reviews due in the UK Amazon marketplace, they could easily do so.

I love this because it gives clarity to authors about where their reviews will end up.

The majority of my royalties come from the US Amazon marketplace. Therefore, this feature is specifically useful for me because now, in the future, if I want to find reviews for the US site, I can filter them out very easily and get those reviews.

Another thing that I absolutely love about this platform is that they offer a 14-day free trial. However, unlike traditional trials on platforms, you usually have to enter your bank details and hope you remember to cancel at the end of your trial if you are not happy with the platform. With Bookbite, you are not required to enter your payment details when signing up. This is a true 'Free trial' in my eyes as users do not need to worry about canceling their account at the end of a trial. This may not be a big thing for you, but I have personally been charged a lot of times when I had forgotten to cancel my membership for a service that I signed up for 14 days prior, so I appreciate this.

Overall, the platform has a lot to offer, I am very impressed with it, and I will continue to share it with my publishing friends. I definitely recommend you try it out, I have not seen something like it in the industry.

Chapter 9: How Will AI Influence Self-Publishing?

It is no secret how powerful AI has gotten in the last few years; ChatGPT has illustrated how smart these machines have really become. In this chapter, I will discuss how I believe AI will influence the self-publishing space in the next few years.

Over the last few months, I have seen a lot of AI books being uploaded to Amazon KDP. Yes, people are now using AI to write books from start to finish. The funny thing is that people want to use AI to write books, but nobody wants to read AI books. It's really easy to differentiate a book written by AI from a book written by an actual human with real emotions. The difference is quite clear to see.

Personally, I am not a fan of self-publishers using AI to write books. It is unethical, lazy, and somewhat tarnishing to this industry. I have never used AI to write a book, and I never will because I don't think AI can ever get to a level where it displays emotion and experience from a writing point of view. Or at least it has yet to reach that stage, anyway.

Currently, it is unclear what Amazon's stance is on AI, as I have seen many newly published AI books be published on Amazon. However, I wouldn't be surprised if Amazon were to ban them in a few months and potentially invest in AI detector software for their back end. This way, they would be able to sniff out any book submissions with AI-generated text. This is my prediction of what will happen, although we can never be sure about anything.

Although, there are things that I do use AI for, and I will explain how you can also use AI as a **TOOL** to help streamline the self-publishing process and make it easier for you (**NOT** for writing books)

Use AI to help you create book outlines

If you have created a book outline for a fiction or non-fiction book, you know how tedious it can be. This is because you have to do a ton of research, read many book reviews from competitors, and generally be clued up to some extent in the niche you are publishing.

Sometimes, I may create a book outline and then ask ChatGPT to also create a book outline for that same book. Then, I will compare my outline with the outline created by AI, and occasionally I may take ideas from the AI-generated book outline and find creative ways to slightly update it and incorporate it in my own outline.

Let me give you an example.

Let's say my keyword for my upcoming book was **"How to Start a social media marketing agency."**

The next step would be how to enter your prompt into ChatGPT. Many people enter lackluster prompts and are surprised when the outcome is undesirable. You have to be very detailed with your prompts to get back something worthwhile.

Let me give you an example of a prompt I may use in this example. I may say, **'Give me a book outline for how anybody can start a social media marketing agency in 2023 with zero capital and no background in advertising and business'.**

'Give me a book outline for how anybody can start a social media marketing agency in 2023 with zero capital and no background in advertising and business.'

Title: From Zero to Social Media Success: The Definitive Guide to Starting a Thriving Marketing Agency in 2023

Introduction:

- The importance of social media marketing in today's digital landscape.
- Addressing common misconceptions and barriers to entry.
- The promise of this book: a step-by-step guide to building a successful social media marketing agency with no capital and no prior advertising or business experience.

Chapter 1: Laying the Foundation

- Understanding the fundamentals of social media marketing.
- Identifying your target audience and niche.
- Setting realistic goals and defining success metrics.
- Developing a personal brand to establish credibility.

Chapter 2: Building Your Skill Set

- Exploring various social media platforms and their marketing potential.
- Learning about content creation, curation, and optimization.
- Developing basic graphic desi

Regenerate response

Chapter 2: Building Your Skill Set

- Exploring various social media platforms and their marketing potential.
- Learning about content creation, curation, and optimization.
- Developing basic graphic design and copywriting skills.
- Utilizing analytics tools to measure performance.

Chapter 3: Creating Your Service Offerings

- Assessing market demands and identifying profitable services.
- Defining your agency's unique selling proposition.
- Crafting compelling service packages and pricing models.
- Designing attractive proposals and contracts.

Chapter 4: Acquiring Clients Without Spending Money

- Leveraging personal and professional networks.
- Utilizing social media platforms for lead generation.
- Harnessing the power of content marketing and thought leadership.
- Implementing referral programs and strategic partnerships.

Chapter 5: Scaling Your Agency

- Outsourcing tasks and building a remote team.
- Developing efficient workflows and project management systems.
- Optimizing client acquisition a Regenerate response
- Upselling additional services to existing clients.

end a message

Chapter 5: Scaling Your Agency

* Outsourcing tasks and building a remote team.
* Developing efficient workflows and project management systems.
* Optimizing client acquisition and retention strategies.
* Upselling additional services to existing clients.

Chapter 6: Navigating Legal and Financial Considerations

* Understanding legal requirements and registering your agency.
* Budgeting and financial planning for a bootstrapped agency.
* Managing client contracts and invoicing.
* Protecting intellectual property and data privacy.

Chapter 7: Continuous Learning and Growth

* Staying updated with industry trends and algorithm changes.
* Networking with peers and attending industry events.
* Seeking mentorship and joining relevant communities.
* Investing in personal and professional development.

Conclusion:

* Recap of key takeaways and milestones achieved.
* Encouragement to take action and start the journey.
* Inspiring success stories of individuals who started from scratch.
* Final thoughts on the future of digital marketing agencies.

As you can see, I did this, and it gave me a very detailed book outline. This was one example of a prompt I came up with in a matter of seconds. If you sat down and thought about your prompt, I'm sure you could have come up with a better one than me. As I said, it's all about being detailed and creative with your prompts.

In the end, you may or may not take ideas and inspiration from the outline created with AI, but in my opinion, giving it a shot is worthwhile.

Use AI to help you come up with a book title

Remember how I mentioned earlier in the book how Amazon's algorithm has changed and is now becoming more of a 'creative' algorithm? Well, if you are not a creative person, you would be missing out if you were not using AI to get ideas for your upcoming book title.

Coming up with a book title can be hard. You don't want to make your title too long, nor do you want it to be too short. You don't want it to be a boring title, nor do you want it to be corny and rude. You want it right in the middle, that nice balance. Another thing you have to consider is that your book title must be free from any copyrighted/trademarked terms. You can check to see if your title has any trademarked terms here - **https://www.uspto.gov/trademarks/search.**

Let's say I wanted to come up with a book title for the example I provided above (regarding starting a social media marketing agency).

One prompt I may give ChatGPT in this instance is: **'Give me book title suggestions for a book about how to start a social media marketing agency in 2023 with no capital and no business experience.'**

As you can see, it gave some great book title and subtitle ideas for this hypothetical book. I could play with it more and make the prompt even more detailed. The better your prompt is, the higher chance you have of getting something that you really like with AI. You can't be generic with the prompts. Otherwise, you will get the same results as everyone else using AI.

Use AI to help you write a book description

If you've ever written a book description, you know it can also be a tedious task. You don't want to come off as salesy, yet you also don't want to be too loose. It's hard and time-consuming to come up with a captivating book description that will help you sell copies of your book.

If you read my previous book, 'How To Successfully Self-Publish A Book On Amazon & Audible', then you know that I like to start my book descriptions usually with a rhetorical question of some sort, usually touching on the customers' pain point. Sometimes, it is hard to come up with that first line in the book description, so I may use AI to guide me with that or to give me ideas of catchy phrases/questions that I can use.

Other times, I struggle to write the bodying paragraphs of the book description. In this case, I will ask AI to write me a book description; I will compare it with what I have written. And often times I take a lot of inspiration from the description produced by AI.

Let me give you an example again.

Let's say I was looking for a rhetorical question at the start of my book description for the hypothetical book about starting a social media marketing agency in 2023. In this case, one prompt I may give ChatGPT is: **'Give me some rhetorical questions to start my book description for my book about starting a social media marketing agency in 2023 with zero capital and no business experience'.**

'Give me some rhetorical questions to start of my book description for my book about starting a social media marketing agency in 2023 with zero capital and no business experience'.

Are you ready to defy the odds and transform your dreams into a successful social media marketing agency? How can an ambitious entrepreneur navigate the dynamic world of digital marketing without any capital or prior business experience? Is it possible to carve your path in an industry dominated by giants? In this compelling guide, discover the secrets, strategies, and uncharted territories that will empower you to build an influential social media marketing empire from the ground up.

As you can see, again, it gives some decent suggestions that I can take ideas from.

Let's say I wanted AI to help me with the whole book description. In this case, one of the prompts I may give it is: **'Give me a book description that attracts readers for a book on the topic of starting a social media marketing agency in 2023 with zero capital and no prior business experience.'**

As you can see again, it gives me a very decent book description that I can alter, take inspiration from and make into my own.

Don't get me wrong. I am not saying that you should copy whatever the AI has given you. No! Rather you should read it, think about ways you can modify it and make it even better, and then use that.

In the end, I think the people that know how to use AI properly will use it as a tool to really make the self-publishing process a lot easier and to free up a lot of time that they can use on something else.

Chapter 10: Selling Your Amazon KDP Account

In this chapter, I will discuss how someone can set themselves up to sell their online KDP business. Selling online businesses has become increasingly popular over the last few years, with many new brokers emerging and viable places where you can sell your online business.

By the way, when I say KDP account, I mean your books. When you sell your business, your books get transferred to the buyer, not your account.

Why would I want to sell my KDP account?

It's a good question. Someone may want to sell their KDP account for various reasons. Let's delve into them a bit further.

KDP accounts have high valuations

A few years ago, you would be lucky to get a 15-20x valuation on your monthly profits. Nowadays, however, I am seeing a lot of KDP businesses selling for 30-40x+ monthly profits. That means people are selling their publishing accounts for 30 times the monthly profit +. That means you will get 2 years and 6 months of upfront income from selling your business.

That certainly does sound lucrative and enticing, as that pay-out can help you to start other ventures and invest in other projects.

I have a good friend who builds up KDP accounts and sells them yearly, and he makes a bloody good living from doing so!

You may want to move on to something else

In my opinion, as lucrative as it is to have a KDP business, people can feel like they want to move on to the next opportunity or project. This is normal, though. Humans don't like doing the same thing repeatedly for years. We like trying new things and challenging ourselves to new levels.

Therefore, selling your KDP business in this instance would be the perfect option, as you will be paid a big cheque to help you start new ventures and bring new ideas to life.

Don't sell your KDP account if you are one of these people.

1. You are someone who does not have a plan or idea of what you want to do with the exit money, and you just like the idea of having a big pot of funds sitting around. I would argue that this is not a good thing to do, as it will likely lead to you procrastinating a lot and possibly becoming lazy as you have that security blanket there.

2. If this is your only source of income that you sustain yourself with or your family. I recommend building up a second stream of income before selling your publishing business so that you are not

constantly stressed about how you will provide or live without income.

Where can I sell my KDP business?

There are multiple online marketplaces where you can sell your publishing business. Although, I will mention the two best ones in my opinion.

Flippa

I have seen more than a dozen KDP businesses being sold on the Flippa marketplace over the last few years. Flippa is a very reputable online business marketplace. They put a ton of security precautions for both the buyer and seller, like using escrow as a payment method. Also, I have heard from people who have sold on Flippa that the customer service is great. They take you through each step of the process and are happy to help you with any concerns.

One thing I don't particularly like about Flippa is that you must pay a one-time setup fee when setting up you're listing. It costs $49. This gives you access to listing your business for three months and has what they call a 'Standard reach'. The problem with this is that it may sometimes take longer than 3 months for you to find the right buyer for your KDP business, so this may be tricky.

Another thing to also consider is that Flippa also has a 'success fee' for when you successfully sell your online business through their platform. The fee changes based on the amount that you sell for. The last time I checked, it was:

- 10% success fee for businesses sold for less than $9,999
- 10% success fee for businesses sold for between $10,000 - 49,999
- 8% success fee for businesses sold for between $50,000 - $99,999
- 6% success fee for businesses sold for between $100,000 - $249,999
- 6% success fee for businesses sold for between $250,000 - $999,999
- 5% success fee for businesses sold for between $1,000,000 - $4,999,999
- 4% success fee for businesses sold for between $5,000,000 - $9,999,999
- 3% success fee for businesses sold for $10,000,000+

As you can see, the success fee reduces the more you sell your company. Although for a sold KDP business, you would probably be looking at 10-6% as a success fee.

One thing that I also don't like about Flippa is that just about anybody can list a business on the platform, there is no real vetting, and nobody asks you for proof of earnings, etc. This means that the marketplace is flooded with thousands and thousands of listings. Of course, not all of them are scams, but I think Flippa needs to take the vetting process much more seriously to prevent possible issues from arising.

Empire flippers

In my opinion, Empire Flippers is where you should be listing your KDP business. Let me explain why I believe so.

For starters, there is no fee to upload your business listing. It is completely free. And your listing will stay as long as you are happy for it to stay. Another thing is that empire flippers have a very strict vetting process, so much to the point that I believe there are only about 150-200 businesses for sale on the platform at a time. When you want to list your business for sale on empire flippers, be prepared to come with a ton of documentation. Some people may not like this, but I think it is a good thing as it gives me peace of mind as a buyer that all listings on empire flippers are legit and that there is nothing to worry about.

Like Flippa, empire flippers also have a 'success fee' or commission when you successfully sell your business through their platform. They are as follows:

- If your business is sold for lower than $700,000, the commission will be 15%
- If your business is sold for between $700,000 - $5,000,000, the commission rate is 8%
- If your business is sold for more than $5,000,000, the commission rate is 2.5%

As you can see, their average commission rates are higher than those of Flippa. This, in my opinion, is the only thing I don't like about empire flippers. If the standard commission rates were 10%, like those of Flippa, this platform would be rated 10/10 for me.

With that said, I do feel like you will have more chance of selling your business with empire flippers, as serious buyers tend to look in that marketplace more than on Flippa.

It has a reputation for being the best online brokerage for selling your online business.

Make sure the following are in place if you want to exit your KDP business

You need to do the following things to be able to get the best valuation for your KDP business:

You need to make sure you are building a BRAND, not just some books

This is possibly the most important thing you need to focus on once you start making decent money from your books. It is very easy to separate a brand from some books on Amazon, and if you want to get the highest valuations possible, you need to make sure you brand your books well, to separate them from your competitors. You can do the following to help you build a brand:

- Have a distinctive feel and look about your book covers. They should have their own identity. Maybe there is something specific about your covers that your readers remember you for. Maybe you follow a certain color pattern? Or maybe you are known for your catchy book titles that spark interest?

- Creating an Amazon author account will help to solidify yourself as an author and build your brand. By giving a short description of your pen name with credentials relevant to your niche, it establishes credibility in the eyes of readers and potential buyers of your business.

- Building an email list is tedious but not necessarily hard. Making sure you have a lead magnet in your book to get your customer's emails and potentially sell them more products or have them become part of your ARC team will help you build a brand and fan base. An email list is very attractive to a KDP account buyer.

Focus on Quality, not quantity

The 80/20 rule states that 80% of your results come from 20% of your work. I have found that this is also the case with self-publishers. Someone who may have published over a thousand titles on Amazon likely makes most of their income from not more than ten books.

If I was a buyer, this would be off-putting for me, I would rather buy an account where the books published are less, but the revenue spread is somewhat more even among the books published. This is because it shows a genuine interest in your books when multiple of them are selling among a small collection, instead of only 1% of your bookshelf making up your income from a large collection of books.

You need to focus on producing the highest quality book, doing a proper launch, running your ads, gaining momentum, and then start looking at publishing more books. The problem with most self-publishers is that they give up too early with one book and think they need to publish thousands to gain traction. This could not be further from the truth.

I've spoken to many self-publishers who have published fewer than ten books but make a healthy income of six figures a year +.

Build up your pen name instead of using a different one each time

This is really important. One of the best ways to build up your KDP brand is to publish multiple books with one pen name. Many self-publishers find a profitable keyword, publish in that niche, and move on to other profitable niches.
Let me give you an example.

Let's say i do my keyword research and conclude that I want to create a book in the OCD niche (obsessive-compulsive disorder). What most people would do in this instance is create that book with a pen name and then instantly move on to a different niche, like gardening, crypto, NFTS, etc with a new pen name.

This is not a smart thing to do because you are not giving yourself a chance to build a real audience of readers who recognize your work. What your goal should be after writing the first book in the OCD niche is to look at sub-topics/branches that are also profitable that you can write books on, such as ADHD, Asperger's syndrome, depression, anxiety, etc.

You should try writing as many books as possible under one pen name, provided the books are all somewhat linked and related, and the keywords are profitable. This is your best bet at building an audience of avid readers.

Conclusion

Thank you for reading this book. If you have not already, I highly recommend you pick up my first book 'How To Successfully Self-Publish A Book On Amazon & Audible' as it will help you with the actual steps of publishing your book.

This book was not intended to teach you how to self-publish. Rather it was written to shed some light on important self-publishing topics. Also, I included some important strategies that will help you to sell your books on a larger scale and become profitable from self-publishing.

Remember that self-publishing is a long-term game, so stay patient and give it your best shot.

If you enjoyed this book and learned some new things, I would really appreciate it if you could leave me your honest review on the product page, as it really helps me out as a smaller author. Thank you, and I can't wait to hear your feedback.